MW01531775

The Journey / The Path

The way I see it

LaDonna Marie

Copyright © 2021 LaDonna Marie.

All rights reserved. No part of this publication may be reproduced, distributed, or transmitted in any form or by any means, including photocopying, recording, or other electronic or mechanical methods, without the prior written permission of the publisher, except in the case of brief quotations embodied in critical reviews and certain other noncommercial uses permitted by copyright law. For permission requests, write to the publisher, addressed "Attention: Permissions Coordinator," at the address below. Scriptures taken from the New King James Version®. Copyright © 1982 by Thomas Nelson. Used by permission.

ISBN: 978-1-63752-356-8 (Hardback)

Any references to historical events, real people, or real places are used fictitiously. Names, characters, and places are products of the author's imagination.

Front cover image by Chima Luke Okafor Back cover image by Shelly Carpenter

First printing edition, 2021

Acknowledgements

To Landon and Lathan, I love you to the moon and back. I would like to thank Adele Brinkley for her superior editing skills, and T.K. Ware was his insightful and hands on approach for the process of this book.

Dedication

To the people who will pick up this book with the desire to follow the Path that God has planned for them. I want to encourage you to continue to keep your hand in his hands.

The Journey / The Path

Note From the Author

I pray that this book will help to assist you in your journey. Trust that God has a plan for your life and trust the process. John 15:16 Ye have not chosen me, but I have chosen you, and ordained you, that ye should go and bring forth fruit, and that your fruit should remain: that whatsoever ye shall ask of the Father in my name, he may give it you.

Scriptures for Mediation

Trust in God

❖ Isaiah 40:31 But they that wait upon the Lord shall renew their strength; they shall mount up with wings as eagles; they shall run, and not be weary; and they shall walk, and not faint.

❖ Psalm 18 I will love thee, O Lord, my strength.2 The Lord is my rock, and my fortress, and my deliverer; my God, my strength, in whom I will trust; my buckler, and the horn of my salvation, and my high tower.3 I will call upon the Lord, who is worthy to be praised: so shall I be saved from mine enemies.

❖ Psalm 91:1 He that dwelleth in the secret place of the most High shall abide under the shadow of the Almighty.

❖ Psalm 18:6 In my distress I called upon the LORD, and cried unto my God: he heard my voice out of his temple, and my cry came before him, even into his ears.

Table Of Contents

During the time close to May 8, 2015
God laid the title

The Journey/ The Path: The Way I See It

Throughout the book, I will share entries from my
notebooks.

CHAPTER 1

The Journey / The Path

The Journey into the Unknown
You have the strength.
within you to journey into
the unknown courageously,

Hold your head up.
Dust your shoulders off.
Stick your chest out.

Set your goals and move forward.
Focus on the journey and
Start to enjoy the path as life unfolds.
One day at a time
LaDonna Marie

In the year 2012, I had a conversation with the Lord about my life. I decided to have a true and transparent talk with Him about my journey and path on this earth. As far back as I can remember, I always talked to God about every aspect of my life. I had been doing this since my teenage years because He does want to hear about what concerns us.

Although He always knows, it sets the scene for deeper intimacy and relationship when we offer to tell Him, even if we find ourselves trembling sometimes.

I knew a healing ultimately needed to take place. I decided that it was time to put an end with the things I could feel in my soul, things God was not pleased with. I investigated areas of my life that I was not happy about in order to do the necessary work to evolve into the woman of God He genuinely wanted me to be. I could always feel God calling me higher.

So, we begin to look deeper into patterns, mindsets, actions, and all things that were comfortable and familiar. I took out a piece of paper and wrote down words that identified these areas. Then, I asked the Lord to help me.

I apologized for all the time that I tried to control my life. The times when I tried to play God and change other people by me just wanting and desiring them to change so badly. I asked for forgiveness for trying to carry a load that was never really mine to carry. I had found this scripture, Isaiah 10:27, that says, "In that day their burden will be lifted from your shoulders, their yoke from your neck; the yoke will be broken because you have grown so fat."

If truth be told, I was not happy with my present circumstances, chaos and so forth. I had my job and starting entrepreneur business things that were going right, yet in this moment, there were still more personal development that needed fixing. I knew that I needed to surrender these things fully to the Lord.

This hard time was the beginning of my era as a divorcee and the life of a single mom. I knew I had to have the Lord on my side to make it through the rough time.

This book is about The Journey/ The Path. The two scriptures that helped me through my hard times told me, "I can do all things through Christ who strengthens me" (Philippians 4:13) and "Greater is he that is in me than he that is in the world" (John 4:4).

These were the ones that I repeated and committed to memory for my everyday life.

When I take time to reflect, I am thankful for the journey, although sometimes, I became disturbed by the time it took to be truly free. Nevertheless, over the years I started to understand that God's plan and God's timing were always best for me. He wooed me to show me a different perspective from all I ever known. He positioned me for His purpose to show me how much I had grown in Him.

He taught me to honor myself as He does. To stop giving discounts to representatives of fake love. To desire wholeness and be free from the enemy's mind games that crushed me mentally. So, with my head held high, I focused on the future. I look to the hills from where my help comes from rather than trying to figure it out instead.

The Bible states that he who has not sinned should cast the first stone. So, we all must repent and forgive ourselves. The path that God is calling us on is a righteous, holy path. It is written be holy as I am holy (1 Peter 1:16). When you begin to look at your life, it's always important to self-reflected, for we are always present on the journey.

God gives instructions, commandments, and examples to follow as He leads us on the narrow path.

The decisions you're making now, and even those you don't make, will help to determine your path. Each day you get a chance to approach the day or not. There is always an option available. I asked myself how do I move forward with everything that God has set up for me to do. It soon become simple for me to let go of my agenda and allow God's will to be done in my life.

Thinking back, I can remember God made himself visible in my low times and struggle. The journey took me through hurt, pain, rejection, fear of failure and being stuck in disbelief. With tears in my eyes, I cried out to God, for He has not brought me this far to leave me now.

CHAPTER 2

Determined to Follow God's Plan

When I was younger, God gifted me with writing to help heal myself and others. It was given at a time when I needed healing the most. I was struggling to find my place in the world because how I felt inside my heart was quite different from how my environment felt. I was born with an innate ability to love others and have compassion for them. I always cared to encourage others even when I needed encouraging.

Because my outlook was always different, I felt as if I did not belong in many places. I wanted to see the good in others and hope for the best in them. That type of thinking was not what my surrounding and being brought up in a small town said.

However, my relationship with God early on calmed me. He always said to me that He validated me and that I did not have to fit in with those who did not want to include me or receive me.

Yet I was still a teenage girl, with a lot of emotions that I could not handle. I had an encounter with God, and He told me that as He had healed me, the words I wrote will heal others. Now, I was between the ages of 12-14, and I believed Him.

I took out my pen and pad and began to write. I wrote all my feelings out and listened closely to what God said. I learned how to be quiet as He spoke and then wrote and typed all the poems down.

I spent most of my days sitting in my room, writing poetry. Although I did not exactly know the full path, I was obedient to God and began to write. When I was brave enough or urged by God to share some of the poems with friends or classmates, I did.

They always said that the poem sounded like something they needed to hear. Or the poems I wrote were as if I knew what they were going through. I always felt comfortable when they would say the poem helped them because the feedback always let me know I was on the right path and listening correctly to God.

My intention always was to make a difference in the world and in the lives of others. When I got a chance to meet the late Dr. Maya Angelou in an airport one day, I stood before her excited and giddy.

I was passionate to tell her how I was a ninth grader reading her books and that I wanted to write books that help others to face their pain and heal.

She smiled and encouraged me to do just that. That was the greatest moment of my teenage life. I carry the memory of that moment with me with every book I write, in order to stay true to God and my goal to impact lives.

My faith in God allowed me to trust Him when He told me that He would make my name great if I always kept Him first and helped others to heal for His glory. God showed me in that time of my life that He would never leave me or forsake me. He would be there when I called and even when I did not. I kept writing even though it took me 12 years to ever publish a first book. I wrote whenever I was inspired so I could be ready when it was time to publish a book.

I had many situations that had happen over the years although I was still changing and evolving. My focus was to help the readers who picked up the book. I wanted to be there for them like God had been there for me, helping them to know they could overcome any obstacles in their paths.

CHAPTER 3

Being Fed up

I can admit
It took me a long time
To learn unconditional
Self love
And I have God to thank.

Being that I write practically everything down, I got quiet and sat at the edge of my bed. I had decided I needed to process some things. There was this paper, right? I jotted down these words on a white legal pad in purple ink. I wrote I had to stop giving into my flesh. I had done a lot of things I am not proud of, so I choose today to repent and live holy. I want my soul to be saved. I want to go to heaven to be with my father. I rebuke lust, loneliness, emotions, and sexual sin.

I then proceeded with another list of abandonment, intimacy, promiscuity, and negative relationship. Then, I circled abstinence, celebrate celibacy. My final thoughts were I just want to stop everything and let God take control, to show Him I trust Him. Lord, I want to be free and clear my mind from the feeling of being emotionally unstable.

I would feel like so much would be going on with understanding life, personal growth and not truly able to be present. I would sometimes always write down my feelings, because it always felt therapeutic to me. On another piece of paper, I had written my thoughts on dealing with rejection. It stated I am not my own, for my life is not my own. If it had not been for the Lord on my side, I do not know how far I would have made it. Looking back but trying to stay in the present, I experienced so many disappointments, setbacks, attacks, and negativity that almost made me attempt to take my life. The pain that I felt back then had convinced me that I should not be here, so I decided I did not want to be here.

I have learned that many times in life that if we get stuck in an experience it is because we need a healing and deliverance on that level. But by placing one foot in front of the other, God carried me. We cannot soar into places that we have not properly prepared to do the work in. Healing was necessary on this level, I had decided to start now to pull back the layers because everything felt too contaminated to move forward. I had so many questions in life, like why this always happened, why did I always pick the same type of guy, what was the root and core issue of my fleeting happiness? I mean I had one question after another because it was truly time to get the healing process started. I really dug deep and looked at myself eye to eye and let God reveal me to me. No more hiding. I was learning to stretch my time to be a full-time single mom, but I really needed to do this work. At that point, it was about leaving a legacy for my children and my children's children.

CHAPTER 4

Mindset Shift

It's important to believe before you see it.
You must have faith.
That it's already there.
Jesus said anything is possible.
If you believe. LaDonna Marie

I AM

Go with me

Take this journey with me

I write broken.

In writing poetry, I am…

I am the misunderstood child

I am the abandoned child

I am the lonely child

I am the neglected child

I am the emotional abuse child.

When I speak I

I am the hurt inside

I am pain

I am the tears that shed

I am the child lost

I am the teen that rebels

I am the chaos that exists within

When I speak, I take on the voice of the people, for

I am the one who overcame

I am the one that decides to live

I am the victorious

I am the peace that is found

I am the reflection

I am the truth

I am joy

I am happiness

I am love

Finally, I am growth.

It started a long time ago, sitting up in my room when the enemy got hot on my trail to sabotage my life. He bombarded me with constant rejection to make me feel that I was not good enough and that something was wrong with me. Not being able to understand fully that he has one goal to kill, steal, and destroy us, and he never takes a day off. I was constantly trying to pick myself back up and keep moving.

This one time, I was so fed up with everything. Thinking no one would miss me, that I was not even liked anyway, I decided to attempt suicide, so I could just get my life over with already. I thought the future was too far ahead, and I could not even imagine waiting to make it that far. All I knew is that I wanted this life right now to be over.

I went forward with the attempt to kill myself, but I could not handle the pain. I crawled to get help, made it to local hospital, and they transferred me in an ambulance to another hospital in next town where they pumped my stomach.

As I laid there on the table with the light shining in my face, I had a visitation for the Lord, and He whispered, "This is not how your story ends, I have more work for you to do."

Right then, I knew, I was destined for great things because He saved my life and allowed me to remain in the land of the living. I started to take pride in the fact that even though the road was not going to be easy, I knew that God would never leave me or forsake me, that He would always be there when times got tough. I just had to cry out to Him to help me on my journey. I rejoiced because that could have been my last day.

He then gave me the gift of healing, and in my writings, I began to help others heal as they overcame their own obstacles. I would be able to testify and let them know that there is nothing too hard for God. He would meet them were they are and help to bring them out. Many times afterwards, the enemy tried to test me with one thing after another to see if I could be pressured enough to go back to that place of wanting to commit suicide. In those times, God always reminded me that He had given His only son to die for our sins, and the victory was already won.

Understanding that the battle was won, my mindset became something that I had to renew daily to encourage myself to keep moving forward. I began to write through my feelings and trust that the Lord would help me to push on.

The mind is the most important part of your body because where the mind goes the body goes also. I begin to repeat affirmations each day and write them everywhere so I could see them, to remind myself how awesome I was even if I were just starting to believe it. God believed I was awesome, and He saved my life that I may have a chance to live and empower others through the poems He was giving me. I knew that my journey was about the people who were waiting to meet me. Although I was going through, learning to believe in who God created me to be, I was overcoming my insecurities to go back and pull others out.

Making the decision to think like God and say what He says about you is so important. I have learned over the years that the enemy will use those who are close to you to cast doubt, fear, pain, and lies about you to get to think less of ourselves. Putting on the mind of Christ is essential because He will always love on you, encourage you, and correct you when needed.

The Bible states that he chastens those whom he loves. As you go through life and in all your day-to-day situations, make sure that your mind is focused on the right things.

Focus on good and positive attributes that can help you to stretch and grow into who God wants you to be.

Just know when you make the choice to do right, evil will always be present. You must resist and choose the right way. Choose the narrow path and not the wide one.

13 Enter ye in at the strait gate: for wide is the gate, and broad is the way, that leadeth to destruction, and many there be which go in thereat. 14 Because strait is the gate, and narrow is the way, which leadeth unto life, and few there be that find it (Matthew 7:13-14).

The enemy seeks to gain control over our thoughts. I have learned we must deny access to the enemy in our minds and choose to think what God says about us. I also apply and plead the blood of Jesus over my life and mind daily, plus the full armor of God found in Ephesians 6:10 -17 **Finally**, my brethren, be strong in the Lord, and in the power of his might.

11 Put on the whole armour of God, that ye may be able to stand against the wiles of the devil.

12 For we wrestle not against flesh and blood, but against principalities, against powers, against the rulers of the darkness of this world, against spiritual wickedness in high places.

13 Wherefore take unto you the whole armour of God, that ye may be able to withstand in the evil day, and having done all, to stand.

14 Stand therefore, having your loins girt about with truth, and having on the breastplate of righteousness.

15 And your feet shod with the preparation of the gospel of peace.

16 Above all, taking the shield of faith, wherewith ye shall be able to quench all the fiery darts of the wicked.

17 And take the helmet of salvation, and the sword of the Spirit, which is the word of God:

When I finally decided to come off the Ferris wheel of crazy highs and lows, and choosing the same spirit just in a different person, I begin to take control of my thoughts by shifting my mind.

Apart of the process was repeating affirmations and writing them in every tablet or piece of paper I could get a hold of; the plan was to be intentional. This is an example of an entry into a notebook:

I am a great mom. I am a great friend. I am healthy.

I have healthy children I am beautiful

I have a successful business. I am kind.

I am an inspiration. I am grateful.

I am healed.

I am a daughter of Zion. I am loved.

I am a child of the Most High. I am blessed.

Keep seeking the Lord's face and build your relationship with Him. Psalm 27:13 reminds me that I would have lost heart unless I had believed that I would see the goodness of the Lord in the land of the living. We must be determined to change our mindset to gain clarity.

CHAPTER 5

Faith Walk

Now faith is the substance of things hoped for, the evidence of things not seen. (Hebrews 11:1)

Hidden Treasures

The press was necessary to bring out

the hidden treasures inside.

To pull down any and everything

that tries to exalt itself against God.

The press will let you know where

you stand in your prayer life and faith.

We must not become weary in well doing.

Although life seems hard

Trouble does not last always,

For God is near all those who call out to him.

I woke up on March 3, 2015 ready to drop another spoken word piece that I had prepared for my Conversations with God Album. I went to work determined to attract positivity with my new Law of Attraction skills. I found myself saying everything good always happens to me. I walked to the bathroom mirror in my daily conversations with God and said, "You know I am a 'momprenuer' and a 'mogul-preneur. Twenty minutes later my VP and Company HR man came in and asked for my cellphone and computer, and I was at home at 12:30 p.m. I was let go; my position had been eliminated.

As I pressed my way inside my house door, I begin to dialogue with God, and I said what do I do, you know I have my two sons. My life had shifted for a moment. I shed a tear when I thought about the road ahead.

He said to me, "Use what you have in your hands." Then, I told God I trusted him. I looked up to Heaven and said, "I hear you." At the time I had books Expressions of the Mind, Body and Soul, and Until Tomorrow Comes. I knew I had to use what He had given me. I knew He meant for me to push the books, and start sharing as He had given me to do many years ago.

Being without a job was so new to me, and I started to feel another moment of uncertainty. I called a close friend, got my feelings in check, and started back on my faith walk. I realized my faith was strong, and I trusted the Lord. I knew He did not bring me this far to leave me. I also knew I had to wake up each day and do my part.

I said to myself, "That in this process, and I will try not to worry." I started looking around and saw so many people making big changes, and I felt the urge to work harder. God sent people who did not know my circumstances to encourage me.

Out of the blue, a friend told me that God had a blessing for me. Trust me, I was ready! In this journey it is crucial that you continue to trust God and have the best attitude. I remember the scripture in 2 Corinthians 1:20 that said all prayers are yes and Amen.

I learned to pray and depend on God to be my Jehovah Jireh (my provider). I prayed that night, went to bed, and woke up the next morning feeling blessed and recharged. I was as confident as I could be. Now, I had to use the gifts that God had for me. I was ready for the overflow.

I started with things that God had placed in my heart to do. I reached out and began to connect with other businesswomen I had met. I dug down deep and found courage I never knew I had. I started on my first book tour to help empower others.

I begin to feel determined to make it and have the successful life that God planned for me. I did not have everything under control, I just knew I had to do something different. In those days, I noticed that I had to rely on God's word, meditation, and prayer were most important.

Some days, I felt so lost, but God kept validating me and keeping me strong. I had to learn to obey God's way.

In that season, I learned the true meaning of the scripture found in Philippians 4:12-13. "I know how to be abased, and I know how to abound. Everywhere and in all things, I have learned both to be full and to be hungry, both to abound and to suffer need."

During the season when I lost my job there were times when I didn't know how I would make it through, with less then what I was used too, but I was thankful. I remembering having to stretch $20 a long way just to buy some things I needed. Then out of the blue God would send people to take us to grab a meal, and I didn't say a word about I needed, He just supplied it.

Also, my car got repossessed and I had to start using public transportation to go to Walmart to shop and even to use a taxi to drive me to go set up to sale books. Through it all, I would say every day I can do all things through Christ who strengthens me.

I learned to trust God for everything during the time with no job. During that moment, He had brought many accomplishments my way. I learned that very year I was a National finalist for a book that was God led and spoken. Which was a struggle due to some spiritual attacks because I chose to start to talk about my suicide story that year. I pushed out Volume one of Quiet Moments with God that I clearly heard Him say write. Then, I put out the Poetry Album on Amazon called Conversations with God. Each day, I had to wake up and trust God.

As I begin to focus on the goodness of God, I decided to go on a trip with a friend. While sitting on the plane, I was saying to myself something good is going to happen. Then I struck up a conversation with a lady who was sitting behind me. We exchange a few words, and I told her that I was and an author and speaker. During our conversation, I secured a speaking engagement while on the plane. The next thing I knew I was speaking for a room full of ladies at a Discover the winner in you Mary Kay Seminar. I learned by expecting blessings to show up in my life, to affirm the greatness God had place on the inside of me through positive energy, and to speak those things that are not as if they are so that great things can happen.

Then on the way back home while waiting in the airport and allowing God to use me, I helped to inspire a young lady about some life decisions that she needed to make and clarify for herself. As we sat there and talked, I was able to help encourage her to feel better about being a leader and confident with her decisions.

To top it all off, I won in the New York Book Festival. During this time, it helps me to stretch my faith, to trust God, and to work hard. My calling was never about getting things from God; it was about surrendering my will to Him, about giving Him control and allowing Him to lead me.

There will be times in our lives when unexpected life troubles happen and catch us by surprise. Just know that they did not catch God by surprise. I was beginning to see that the favor of God was surrounding me. I was trusting in God for everything. I woke up one morning, by the referral of my Pastor at the time , to an opportunity to do a TV interview. This was my first time on a Christian Broadcast. I was thankful, even though I had to keep pressing. God continued to show that He was Faithful.

We must continue to seek His face in our frustrations and let Him guide our footsteps. I truly learned that with God all things are possible. There's nothing too hard for God. We must allow Him to have total control.

CHAPTER 6

Settle No More

I am woman.

I am woman, hear me roar

I am strong because

I've been weak I am resilient because

I've gone through

I am powerful because I've been restored

I am persistent because I have preserved through every obstacle that landed on my path.

I am woman, hear me roar

I am fearless because I dug deep to find my voice.

I am excited about my future because I have closed the door to my past.

I am beautiful because I chose To shower myself with self-love.

I am confident because I choose to believe in myself and dismiss the opinion of others.

I am woman, hear me roar.

I am victorious because I focus on my destiny.

I will succeed because the word says if God is within her, she will not fail.

I made a conscience decision to settle no more in relationships. All the relationships I had ever been in, I went into them thinking that I was responsible for everything. I was the one who could help them to change if I just kept being supportive. But all the while, these relationships made me feel terrible on the inside.

I felt like I had to push myself to the limit in order to do everything I could to make something happen, only to have that same feeling of emptiness on the inside each time the relationship didn't work.

As far back as I can remember, I looked for love in all the wrong places, in places where it did not exist. It took me a long time to break the cycle of pushing myself to depletion in order to make someone else happy, while I felt like I was dying. It was like I kept bumping my head until I just said enough is enough. Then, God was like, "Let me have this time with you because I love you."

Through my life in every relationship, I could always sense and feel that God was there in my corner, telling me He loved me and showing me just how much as He saved me from situations. I wrote in my journal: Am I settling? Things are not going how I expected.

I always felt like, if I could just get them to see I loved them how much, then maybe they would love me in return. If I would just bend over backwards to do all of this and that, everything would be good. My life was like a revolving door of different relationships, but always with the same outcome.

God waited for me, He loved on me. He did not shun me for the times I messed up. He welcomed me with open arms. He taught me I did not have to give my body for people to love me, and I did not have to be mistreated and talked down too. He showed me in the Bible that my body was bought with a price and that it was the temple of God and should remain holy.

He taught me to respect myself, for I was the apple of His eye and a daughter of Zion. He taught me that I was royalty, a queen, and should be treated as such. I did not have to be afraid of wanting to be in a monogamous relationship. It was ok to wait on the person that He had chosen for me, and he would be worth the wait.

God taught me to take sex off the menu and to obey all the commandments, not just some. It took some time, but I was tired of the constant drama, empty promises, verbal, emotional, and mental agony that I had placed myself in by trying to make relationships work that should not.

I decided to go all in with God because He genuinely wanted what was best for me. This time with Him helped me to get rid of soul ties with people and to be free to start to choose me. I wasn't going to rush into another relationship until God said the man is my purpose partner. After bumping my head so many times, I wanted to be able to learn how to love myself truthfully and honestly. It was a time of healing—a time to replace every lie the enemy told me that no one was going to ever want me, a time to work on myself, and a time to be positioned with the right mindset as I devoted my time to the Lord and the ministry of advancing the kingdom. It was a time to learn self-love, and how much God loved me.

In past relationships, it was not that I had given up on people. Instead, I gave up on settling. I decided how and what capacity I would live. So, my story is not about other people, but it is about the lessons of strength and endurance to discover my identity.

I decided to no longer be hurt or in a pain by what others gave out. Mostly, I wanted to be defined by who God wanted me to be, to learn from each experience, and to continue to seek the love and care the Father has for me. I embraced this season as I waited for a love that God will send me in due time.

In this season, I choose to choose me first. I have had a rough couple of years with relationships and love. Now I choose me to help to evolve.

On August 16, 2015, I wrote in my journal, "I will celebrate life. Today, I will celebrate happiness. Today, I will no longer accept what no longer serves me. I am worth the wait. I am delivered and healed through Jesus Christ and covered with His blood. I will no longer tolerate what I don't like."

CHAPTER 7

Encounters

My life has always been unique, starting when I began to hear the voice of the Lord. I built a relationship slowly and learned how to yield to the Holy Spirit. In John 16:13 states, "But when he, the Spirit of truth, comes, he will guide you into all the truth. He will not speak on his own; he will speak only what he hears, and he will tell you what is yet to come."

Although most of my life, I did not have language for what I was experiencing; however, I knew it was God and was excited about listening and being obedient. Most of my life, when I started to write all my books, I learned to listen as the Holy Spirt downloads and to have the pen of the ready writer. In 1998 my feelings on relationships, love spirituality, healing and guidance, was what God had pressed upon my heart to share. I had never really heard people talk about the Holy Spirit and what His purpose is on Earth, so I thought I was going to be looked at as weird if I told people, I was able to hear and understand. Moreover, that I had been listening and following Him and He helped me to know that part of my purpose was to help others to heal; using what God gave me to share with them.

I took a trip to California in 2013 and met some mighty men and women of God and gained brothers and sisters in Christ. While there, I felt like I was on a spiritual sabbatical. It was there the

Lord introduced me to men and women of God, who helped with language for my life.

They helped me to understand my life and its journey. In 1 Timothy 4: 14, we read, "Do not neglect your gift, which was given you through prophecy when the body of elders laid their hands on you." Words I needed to hear.

This happen to me: In the church in California, where hands were laid on me, and my head was anointed, God spoke and called me an evangelist. Then, my whole life made sense. Before then everywhere I went by the leading of the Holy Spirt, I shared the good news about Christ, or the word of God was how conversations went with others as I traveled at my tables selling books. While on that trip, the Holy Spirit spoke to me about Planting Positive Seeds, my nonprofit to help with His children to learn more about His will for them.

I had never conducted a conference, but I followed the instructions of the Lord, returned home and started to plan. It was like I had been catapulted into doing the will of God and all that He wanted me to do for Him. The conference was amazing. It was a Youth for Christ Conference that helped to empower those who has gone through obstacles and encourage them on ways to keep moving forward.

Also, that year I was writing my second book Until Tomorrow Comes, and it was so important for me to yield and do it exactly how the Holy Spirit guided. If I would've had it my way, I wanted to jump into erotica. All of my poet friends were erotica at the time. I mean I had even picked out a pseudonym name and shared some poems with my co-workers at the time. Yet, the Holy Spirit told me I could not, so I put the poems aside and they were never used. Everything about this Until Tomorrow Comes was different; I consulted the Holy Spirit on everything. This book focused on choosing everyday situations that we must surrender to God's will or continue to follow our own. He helped me chose the name and how the sections were put together. He wanted Until Tomorrow Comes to be a journey of growth and awareness. God wanted them to know that He would never leave or forsake them, but they would come a time when they would have chosen a path.

The next year, my pastor at the time asked us to make a list of things that we needed God's help and assistance with and to start decreeing and declaring it daily. I wrote down eight needs and started to decree and declare in the mirror daily, and by May of 2014, I was an International Award-winning author in Paris. I immediately gave God thanks for all He had done. The reason of the book was to give God glory and to share the journey of growth and awareness in life. I learned in my obedience to doing the book as He instructed that all the glory was His, for I was the vessel, He used to get the book in the earth.

The call

I can remember in November 2014 my children and I were in church. I was praising the Lord, speaking in my heavenly language, really seeking His face. I heard him say, "I am calling you out. I am here, my child." I immediately stopped and said, "No, God. I am not fully ready."

Knowing I was scared and afraid to step up completely at do all that He was asking me to do, I continued to hide and quietly do the work of the Lord because I did not know fully about my gifts of the Holy spirit and how they worked. (1 Corinthians 12: 8-11, and Romans 12:4-8 Concerning Spiritual Gifts)

After I got back from California, the desire to speak in tongues and speak directly to God grew. I was at home one day, and I cried out (prayed and talked) to the Lord, seeking Him and desiring to be filled with the Holy Spirit. Within twenty minutes of praying, crying out, and praising God, out of nowhere, I spoke in tongues. I was overjoyed because I truly desired to have help from the Holy Spirit to fulfill my God given purpose.

Even though I was not fully knowledgeable, I did not stop allowing Him to lead me. I read my Bible and learned how to hear God through studying scriptures. Sometimes, on my way to work or any event, I prayed that God would send the people who needed what He had given me to give, and then people would show up needing prayer and encouragement, all orchestrated by the Holy Spirit. I found myself being led to pray for others and typed prayers and send to those who I heard to pray for. One time I felt the Holy Spirit was asking me to pray for a friend because her name came up in my spirit. So I wrote out the prayer that He gave me. It was almost midnight, and I was too tired to send it, so I prayed it in the atmosphere that it God would send it to where she was. The next day, I saw on her Facebook page that there was a fire next door to her home, and she was praising God for safety. I later contacted her and sent the prayer that I had written. Because of her testimony, I give God all the glory for protecting their lives.

There were days when faces of people flashed before my face. In that moment, God would give me prayers to pray and send to them. One time on a Saturday, while I was at home reading scriptures and talking to the Lord, a woman's face from the church appeared before me. The next day I went to church, sat down on my row and was praying with my head down. When I lifted my head and opened my eyes, the lady was sitting next to me. I said, Lord I will just pray for her from here. I wasn't ready to lay hands in that moment, I just knew God was asking me to pray. Then she got up and walked on her cane to the front. I knew she was seeking God for a miracle. The guy beside me said, I don't know what kind of gift you have, but I was just praying, and I saw my hands in your hands and you were praying. I then begin to understand I was to intercede in the Name of Jesus for healing of people.

I remember going to a conference, and wanted to go to the altar for prayer, but all I had to give was change and no dollars. I was a little embarrassed, but decided to go ahead and give God what I had from my heart. I needed a word from God and wanted to hear what He was saying for my life. I went to the altar, and I met a woman of God there who prayed for me. She said, "God is waiting on you to perform His miracles, signs, and wonders."

I left there encouraged, ran home to my notebook, and looked at all the times that I had written things down. I had seen the hand of God move as people came back to give a praise report about what the Lord had done in their lives. I wholeheartedly believe in the word of God as given in Mark 16:17, "And these signs will accompany those who believe."

It was always important to God and me to see people healed and delivered. There were times when the encounters that I had were not always for others, but they were always for me. The Holy Spirt will bring you into all truth, meaning that God will correct you before or while you're doing something that does not line up with His purpose.

Often, I could see and feel the changes when my prayer life and studying God's word were less. One time, my oldest was playing a sport, and I felt that the coach were a little harsh. I really wanted to go off on him. But in that moment, I kept asking for God to order my words. To be honest, I fired back a little, but not much. The next morning, I heard God say, "Daughter, this is how you should have addressed him." That was the same week that God had given me the name for this book, which happened May 2015.

However, I learned in those days that totally relying on the word of God, mediation, fasting, and prayer is what is most important. I recall the time after I lost my job, and things were tight. I remember sitting on the steps of my townhome, looking up to heaven, and praying to God to help me to understand my journey. Even in those times, the Holy Spirit pressed upon me that my job for the kingdom was to serve others. There was times when I wanted to feel depressed about my own situation. However, I still had to go to my prayer closet and intercede for those whom He laid on my heart. I still had to grab my table and go stand out and sell books, praying that the people who needed what God had given me would come by. One day, the Holy Spirit asked me to get up, take my table, and go sell books. I went, but before I left, I posted to say where I was if anyone wanted to come buy a book.

Some people saw that I would be there and came and bought some books. I was giving God the glory when a young man came by. He said he was supposed to be going the other way, but God brought him my way. We talked, and the Holy Spirit used me and a story to help the young man. He was incredibly grateful that he had come that way, and so was I. The key is to always be sensitive to the leading of Holy Spirit.

CHAPTER 8

Healing

Abba Father,

Search my heart and take out whatever is not like you. Help me to gain and retain the knowledge that is necessary for my next level. God, I want to pour out my cup and ask you to fill me up, so I can be ready for the next season, new life, and new promises. God, I need you and cannot make it without you. I just want to do all you have called me to do to help others to heal and know who they are. Search my heart, God, and remove anything that is not like you. Amen

Make peace with the pain

The first thing God made clear to me is that He had to heal me first and the words that I wrote for others would help to heal. I immediately knew that painfully or not I had to go through a healing. I was healing from anger, sadness, rejection, low self-esteem, doubt, persecution, and words that had been said by others. We must no longer operate from a place of brokenness. Healing is available. As we go throughout life, we must begin to heal broken pieces. The first way we do that is through identifying what you need healing from. I had to go to God and ask him to help me let go of all the things that tied me to my past, to cleanse me and wash me over. According to Psalm 51: 7 Purge me with hyssop, and I shall be clean: wash me, and I shall be whiter than snow.

I had to ask God to help me to forgive even if I did not get an apology. I had to deal with the issues that would try to come back and visit when I was alone.

I wanted to stop every generational blood line curse that wanted to keep me held back in bondage. I wanted to surrender my will to God so that He could use my life to bring him Glory. I had to look myself eye to eye in the mirror and ask God to expose all the wounds of unforgiveness, heart break, and lies that I had caused as well. In the healing process, we cannot always point fingers because we must understand that we signed up for some of the drama too.

God did not tell us to go and do what we did even though we thought we knew better, which we do not.

In making peace within myself, I had to know that with God all things are possible. I'm talking about being rooted and grounded in who He is so that you could have a road map for the journey ahead. I started to pick up my Bible and read and study the scriptures about what He says concerning different topics. I begin to read the story of Job, and in Psalm how David felt and cried out to God. Proverbs, the book of wisdom, teaches biblical truths for day-to-day living.

I had to learn what love really means, that it is patient, it is kind, and it does not remember faults (1 Corinthians 13 4-8). All of the things I learned were teaching me as I begin to seek God more, not for material things, but to get the living water so that I would never have to thirst again.

I spent time in my prayer closet, on my knees, asking God to help me, guide me, lead me, and heal me. After I had tried everything else to fill voids, He was the only solution to all of my issues and fears. The scripture that kept me comforted during rough times was Psalm 147:3, which tells us that He heals the brokenhearted and binds up their wounds. I allowed God to do for me what nothing or no one else could do.

Each encounter with God taught me more and more that I was connected to something bigger than just me.

Although I had to learn I was more than my experiences, I came to the realization that I was enough in God's eyes no matter what anyone else said, and that by going through the process, I was getting set up for my destiny. Each day, I had to choose to walk in His strength, and to realize that I was born for a purpose. I had to work out my own salvation, in order to heal and tap into my true purpose. **It is written in Matthew 16:24** Then said Jesus unto his disciples, If any man will come after **me**, let him deny himself, and take **up** his **cross**, and follow me.

Losing loved ones

It is written in Psalm 30:5, "Weeping may endure for a night, but joy comes in the morning." Dealing with losing a loved one for me was a touchy area for a while. I had to take a deeper look at death and grief. Although it is never easy to lose a loved one, I had to see how much God loved them, and it was His plan to call them back at any time. We are on borrowed time, for tomorrow is not promised.

It's best to go to the scripture and see what it says about death. In James 4:14 it is written, "You do not even know what will happen tomorrow. What is your life? You are a mist that appears for a little while and then vanishes." Also reading the word I learned that in

1 Thessalonians 4:13 "But I would not have you to be ignorant, brethren, concerning them which are asleep, that ye sorrow not, even as others which have no hope." A few people who passed away affected me, but God ultimately showed me the beauty in the relationship.

In college I had a friend and we had become friends quickly. She was a nice person, very smart and kind. I was independent, had leadership skills and loved people. We both needed something from each other. One night we were planning to go to the club, right as we begin to drive off campus, we got into a car accident and were hit by a drunk driver. My head hit the windshield, the driver of our car had mild injuries, and my friend passed away instantly. I was rushed to the hospital and I was foggy for a little while, but I wrote her this when I could remember.

I wrote: First and foremost, friend I love you. Something I never got to say but felt so deeply. Yes, we, we had just met, but you were what I needed in a friend and I was for you. At your funeral I couldn't say goodbye properly because I didn't have my memory. But after months of agony and trying to remember I did and missed you so much. We would have had many happy days as friends. I never asked God why, but I often wanted to. I just seek to look for the positive and good reasons, influence you had on my life in such a short time. I'll never say goodbye, I will hold on to a piece of you forever. God had a reason for your life, and it was not in vain. You made me realize so many things I could change in the months I knew you. You will always be in my heart. I thank God for making it possible for us to meet and come together.

Love Donna

In my journal I wrote: Over the last week I had some visions and memories about people that had passed away. I remember soul-searching about the wisdom of life. When I asked for clarity on what was going on, the Holy Spirit said to go get a journal and I started to write everything that He downloaded. On 8/8/2014, I was walking to my office speaking about my grandmother's personality and her strength. I usually stay yielded every day, so this was normal. In my spirit, it was as if God was preparing me for her passing. Then I asked God to help me to understand what He told me, because I understand we all receive things on different levels. So, I got a text. I assumed they was calling to say she passed. Early the next morning, I got the call that she has passed that morning.

That was a hard time to process, because we a lifetime of memories passed before me. Yet at this time I learned to trust God in all things. Later, I got a call and was asked to do the family tribute at the funeral, and I immediately said yes, because God was already preparing me, and it was practically already written.

Looking at the word, God is saying that tomorrow is not promise. I'm not saying that losing the person and knowing this scripture will make you feel better instantly. God always wants us to cast our cares on Him because He cares. I learned that God wants us to focus on the good times we had with the departed loved ones so we will not grieve for long. It was never His intention for us to carry the sadness and pain with us for years. I look at the situation like this: God gave His only Son to die on the cross for us to be able to live and have life abundantly. So, it is important to repent, live righteously, and know for sure we will be with Him in Heaven.

Being Free

The choice to be free is to seek God's approval and not people. We must align your mind and thoughts with the word of God. The Bible tells us we are not of the world. According to (John 17:14-16,

14) I have given them your word; and the world has hated them, because they are not of the world, just as I am not of the world. 15) I do not pray that You should take them out of the world, but that You should keep them from the evil one. 16) They are not of the world, just as I am not of the world.

The real choice is to be reminded that our purpose is the key to being our authentic selves. Life begins only when we put God and His will for our lives first. When we accept the free gift of salvation that Jesus Christ offers, we are redeemed by his blood. It is written in John 8:36 "If the Son therefore shall make you free, ye shall be free indeed." That means we are free through our confess and belief and we have to walk the path of righteousness. If we fall repent and get back up again.

Coming out of Chaos and Confusion

We must start by denying the enemy entry into our minds. The Bible states that the devil prowls around like a roaring lion looking to see whom he can devour. Be sober minded and alert and understand when we are being tempted to be pulled into the area of distractions and confusion. God is not the author of confusion but of peace.

Life's Lessons

Do not allow your emotions to cause you to retreat. Being emotional unstable has caused me to make a lot of decisions that were not helpful. On this journey I had to learn how to let word of God be my assistance on how to walk this path out. In a 2009 journal entry I wrote: I feel very sad most times. My circumstance is always negative or perceive that way all my life. I have to deal with the overwhelming feeling that I'm not good enough or everything is wrong. It's hard to get a word in where you are constantly judged, criticized and then are supposed to move on like nothing ever happen or nothing was said. It cripples me and hurts my feelings, like nothing I do is good enough. I need help, guidance, strength to move. I'm thankful for grace, mercy and daily favor God gives me.

We should trust God in the middle of constant adversity when destruction is zeroing in on every side. When your head feels as it is under water, I have learned that you must focus your eyes on God, and tell yourself that if God be for you, then who can be against you? 1 Peter 1:13 reminds us, "Wherefore gird up the loins of your mind, be sober, and hope to the end for the grace that is to be brought unto you at the revelation of Jesus Christ.

CHAPTER 9

Embracing Kingdom Identity

God I thank you for having mercy on me

Although times I know I fall short

You still love

Thank you for forgiving my iniquities

And not giving me what I deserved

My spirituality is so important to me. I have known all my life something was special about me. I experienced a lot of encounters with God and miracles and wonders that were unexplainable to a younger me. I travelled many years feeling something was missing, chasing apologies I would never get, and looking for love in all the wrong places. All to have God come a whisper to me that He was all I needed and for me to stop looking around in the secular world for what it could never give me.

Time and time again, I had to learn the lesson to depend on Him totally. I had to understand that my life was never going to be perfect. Each day I am learning how to align my path with His ways and lean not to my own understanding because everything I have tried has not worked at all. Now, I depend on Him, for He is my way maker, and He has kept me, and He loves me just as I am.

Around 2009, I started to read a book by Joel Osteen, and he asked the readers to write the great things that God had done for them. I started to write, and I listed about eighteen blessings. I was grateful that He has saved my life from attempting suicide and my child's life, from falling out the crib. On the list I wrote that He had covered and protected me in 4 car accidents, He wakes me up each day, He helped me finished grad school. All of these things were great chances to give God praise.

Writing the list helped me to shift my focus to the things that God had done for me. At the end of the page, I thanked God for helping me to understand what battles to fight.

I always have talks with God, out loud and in my notebooks too. I wrote, "My soul is being cleansed! God is in control of my life. I am learning to heal and to let go and let God. I want happiness in my life. Look into my heart and keep my actions pure and holy. Continue to shield me from evil and temptations." Thank you for the crown of favor, for covering me each day with grace and mercy. Help me to develop a prosperous mindset of increase, allow me not live-in fear, condemnation or to question my faith.

As I dug deeper in my relationship, God began to fight all my battles. He taught me to trust in Him. I wrote in 2017 God has been showing his mighty hand in my life. I have prayed and committed my focus back to His will completely. I'm increasing my praying and fasting, and He brought a blessing my way I was so thankful to be seeking the kingdom first as declared in Matthew 6:33. "But seek ye first the kingdom of God, and his righteousness; and all these things shall be add unto you."

In this season it is very important that I continue to give God a yes and trust where He leads me. I have always trusted the God of the Bible to be that same, today, yesterday and forever. I remember one day I was at work and a friend's face fell in my spirit and I stopped and prayed. The next day she came to my office out of the blue and said to me the tumor was gone. I immediately gave God the glory. I came home one night and there was a church program that I almost didn't go to. Then my friend texted me and we decided to go. I started feeling pains in my lower stomach, so I went to the altar and prayed for the friend. Later I found out they were in an accident. I have learned to stay connected and yielded to Holy Spirit to be able to discern the will of God.

CHAPTER 10

Radical Obedience Moments

Hello God,

This is your daughter coming to you to ask that you grace me once again to be able to hear and see in the spiritual realm. My one desire is to do what you will have me to do in this season. To ask you to speak to me and grant me the honor of hearing you and the revelation knowledge from heaven. I repent of my sins that have caused me to disobey and not hear from you. I ask that you remove all distractions in this season. Please, God, grace me with discernment to understand you and to prophecy in this season. In Jesus name, Amen.

Your daughter,

Seeking Christ

It is so important to have a relationship with Christ, especially in this time and age. In my life, there was always a need to give thanks to Jesus Christ for the sacrifice He made on the cross for me. I would fall on my knees, and most time, my eyes welled up with tears because I was so grateful that even after all He had been through, He decided that He would give His life to save ours from the penalty of sin. By giving His life, He was fulfilling the love of the Father.

I would often find myself in awe of His love for you and me. As I grew deeper in my faith and placed on the mind of Christ, I had to learn how to seek Him. Many Scriptures, such as Philippians 2:5-7 (KJV) 5 Let this mind in you, which was also in Christ Jesus: 6 Who, being in the form of God, thought it not robbery to be equal with God: 7 But made himself of no reputation, and took upon him the form of a servant, and was made in the likeness of men.

His sacrifice made me give honor and be so grateful that He was obedient even to death. Over the years, as I went through different hardships, I thought about what Jesus would do about concerning the situation and what does the Bible say about it.

Then and only then, was I able to overcome the hard times that were going on in my life because Jesus was my biblical champion. He overcame every obstacle that was placed in His way.

Seeking Him was a part of my path as I started to learn how to win with His life. Even the times when I strayed, I knew that I could repent, turn from wickedness, and stick to the narrow path, for Jesus Christ is the way, the truth, and the life, and we cannot get into the Kingdom without going through Him.

I know that life happens to us all, and in those times, reading the Bible and learning that Jesus is now seated on the right-hand of the throne, and making intercessions for us gives me peace. I feel confident that even when I do not know what to pray, Jesus is praying for me.

I wake up each day knowing my faith is renewed, and that if I have another breath, there is meaning in my life. Jesus said in John 15:5, "I am the vine, ye are the branches: He that abides in me, and I in him, the same bringeth forth much fruit: for without me ye can do nothing."

You see, along the way, there were circumstances that challenged me to want to give up and not press forward. Yet I pressed on because I knew that my destiny was decided, according to 2 Timothy 1:9 "Who hath saved us, and called us with a holy calling, not according to our works, but according to His own purpose and grace, which was given us in Christ Jesus before the world began."

Seeking Christ is also having a relationship with Him, meaning it must be a personal one. I can remember one of my first memories of worshipping and lifting my hands to praise Him. To my surprise, I was called a hypocrite. I was about four or five years old, and out of my mouth came the scripture found in Matthew 19:14, "But Jesus said, Suffer little children, and forbid them not, to come unto me: for of such is the kingdom of heaven." Being that young and having a love for Christ was and still is an amazing memory for me. I realized then that He had chosen me and loved me enough to make sure my zeal for Him was not snuffed out.

I can honestly say that I love Christ, and desired for a long time to follow and pattern my life after Him, and that meant seeking Him and His face. I had to seek Him diligently to find Him so that I could separate myself from the world and be transformed into His image. As I grew in Christ and started to establish our relationship, I had to allow the wisdom of how He lived His life to be my guide.

Building my relationship with Christ allowed me to grow in my faith and trust. Many times, I had to pray for the strength that He said was available. In my life, truly feeling His presence in every one of my decisions, helped me to stay strong when the world seems like it presses you to stay connected to it. Many times, I had to walk up to the altar and cast my cares on Him because He cares for us.

I can say that I truly have grown in seeking Christ and to know that my life was bought with a price and that He is the reason I get another chance. When I felt lost, He was the first person I called on to lead me back to the place I was destined to be. Whenever I felt that life was doing me a disservice, I thought about when He said in John 15:18, "If they hate you, remember they hated me first." My life and hopefully yours will change for the better by truly trusting and seeking Christ to make an impact on your life forever.

CHAPTER 11

The way I see it

I learned that in my life, the Holy Spirit was guiding me in the way that God wanted me to go, think, and behave. As I read the Bible and begin to know the heart and mind of Christ.

As I reflect on my life from age 14 until now, I know that the Holy Spirit came to instruct me toward the path that God had planned for me. Even as a young teen, I did not have language, but I had obedience, and there was just knowing inside of me that following Jesus was the right way to go, even when it was hard. As you have read, there were unpleasant experiences in my life, yet Matthew 6:33 reminded me, "But seek ye first the kingdom of God, and his righteousness; and all these things shall be added unto you."

So, I am ending the book by sharing some insights and revelations that the Holy Spirit taught me. I want you to know, I learned this early, "For our struggle is not against flesh and blood, but against the rulers, against the authorities, against the powers of this dark world and against the spiritual forces of evil in the heavenly realms." (Ephesians 6:12)

When I agreed and partnered with God to help Him heal others through my writings, the enemy launched an attack on me because I was going to encourage others through the trials and victories in my life for the Kingdom.

The Holy Spirit helped me to learn to take a deep look at my broken heart as a teenager and learn where it originated. He helped me to take a deeper look at reasons and not to settle for superficial explanations and how to get to the root of it.

The Holy Spirit gave me another revelation of the reason why my mouth was muzzled. It was by wearing the belt the truth as described in Ephesians 6:14. He showed me how agents of the enemy surrounded me and caused me not to be joyful, thereby letting doubt set in and how I was a threat to the enemy's camp. In discovering this aspect, I can see why the process was so trying at times. Nevertheless, I always trusted God to protect me and be there when I needed Him. I can honestly say I can look over my life and see how He has kept me and saved me from many accidents and attacks that were sent my way. According to Psalm 91:11 For he shall give his angels charge over thee, to keep thee in all thy ways.

Throughout my life on this journey, from the first encounter with the Lord, He has sent men and women of God to confirm His word and promises that He gave me when I was younger. It is refreshing to look back over my life and see that He has never left me. Of course, during some tests and trials, He was silent, yet He was still with me. Psalm 139:8 says, "If I go up to the heavens, you are there; if I make my bed in the depths, you are there."

I am grateful that even when I felt alone, He left the Holy Spirt as a comforter to encourage me to push and press toward the mark of the high call. John 14:16 says, "And I will pray the Father, and He will give you another Helper, that He may abide with you forever." When I learned these truths, the path got easier because God always wants us to know He will never leave us or forsake us. In fact, He said it many times throughout the Bible.

The last revelation He gave me was helping me realizing that I had everything I needed all along to do what he needed me to do and to be the best version of my authentic self, whom He created me to be.

I also realized the enemy's job was always to make me think I had no purpose, and that I was not enough. Those attacks allowed me to understand that I was anointed and just who God created me to be is the main reason God pursued me relentlessly. All I must do is to trust Him and the gifts that He has given me to complete the assignment I was born into this world to complete.

I learned God was preparing me for something great. It is written, In Jeremiah 1:5, "Before I formed you in the womb, I knew you; Before you were born, I sanctified you." I was just that important that He thought about me before I was formed, so He took time to form me in the way that He wanted me to be.

Being able to see my journey from God's viewpoint helped me to see how much He loved me when He gave His only begotten Son so that I might have life. It has taking me spending time in reflection to see just how much Jesus loved us that He gave His life for us.

So, this journey and path have never been about winning awards. Although the picture on the cover is when I won International Author of the Year in London, UK. The smile in that moment, was the assurance that God knows my name. I was nominated for the Divas of Colour 2018 Author of the Year.

I made it to the finalist, list and I was so excited. I had a conversation with God in 2014, when I won my first Honorable Mention in the Paris book Festival for Poetry Book Until Tomorrow Comes. I said that if I even win internationally again I wanted to travel. I ended up having to raise funds to make it that year to San Francisco. I did a Go fund me campaign to assist with the ticket and stay while I was there. When I made it off the plane and was getting a taxi to my hotel, I found out it was an hour away from airport longer than I thought, plus $100 dollars both ways so I lost it. I had to ride a monorail for the first time, and I had to sleep in airport to be able to catch my flight back the next morning.

About 4 years had passed, I had won other awards in between, writing exactly what God asked me to write and I decided that I wanted to go to London, UK. I said to the Lord I was already a winner in my book in my heart, by writing Lessons II: Mirror Conversations, Children's book Larry the Alligator Makes Friends and being placed on the finalist list. I was going whether I actually won or not strictly for the honor. I got there and was 1 out of 3 people from the United States, totally honored just to be there. We didn't know who the winners were yet, my friend and I took pictures and enjoyed ourselves. In a brief conversations we made friends with the photographer there and set at the table with him and his friends. The night went on and everyone looked fabulous. The organizer of the event and I had known each other since 2014 when I was first featured in her husband's magazine in Issue 6 Volume 2.

The moment was here, and they called all the names in the category , then my name was announced as the winner. I was like did I hear correctly, as I walked to the stage I gave God glory, for keeping His promise to the fourteen-year-old girl on the inside, when He said I would go to nations. So the picture on the cover was divine timing that the event photographer caught me basking in the love of God. Each award was always to give God glory with my life and to impact lives and help encourage others for the Kingdom.

It has been a bumpy yet amazing journey. I am so thankful and joyful because I know and believe God will take care of me. He is providing opportunities and blessings. I am embracing the greatness God has placed on the inside. Lastly, I want what God wants for me. The Bible states that He is no respecter of persons, what He does for one He can do for all. Trust in God, and Know You were born with and for a purpose.

Tools for the journey

- Always put God first.

- Have Faith in God's plan for your life.

- Learn how to live righteous.

- Preserve and Stand firm during the trial.

- Have endurance during hard times.

- Learn how to abase and abound.

- Have Hope Always.

- Believe and you will receive.

- Trust in God's timing.

Books by the Author

- Expressions of the Mind, Body and Soul

- Until Tomorrow Comes

- Lessons Shattered Pieces Being Restored

- Quiet Moments with God: 31 days of Life Lessons

- Eloquent Love Notes

- Lessons II Mirror Conversations

- Rebuilding Fragments Workbook

- Larry the Alligator: Makes Friends

- Quiet Moments with God: 21 Days of Positive Inspirations

- Maximizing Your Inner Strength Workbook

- Things I wish I Knew: Letters to My Little Sisters

All books can be purchased at www.ladonnamarie.org/shop

About the Author

LaDonna Marie is an International Multi-Award Winning Best-selling Author, Pastor, Speaker, Mother of Two, and CEO of Nonprofit Planting Positive Seeds. Her purpose is to empower and encourage others in overcoming obstacles in life.

LaDonna Marie assists individuals in transforming their lives through personal development and implementing resiliency skills with her books and her nonprofit organization. Her motto is to empower, encourage, and motivate others to act in their life and discover their champion inside. It is a part of her mission to reach individuals all over to the world and to assist them to LEAP into their greatness.

Journal Entries

Habakkuk 2:2-3

2 And the LORD answered me, and said, Write the vision, and make it plain upon tables, that he may run that readeth it.

3 For the vision is yet for an appointed time, but at the end it shall speak, and not lie: though it tarry, wait for it; because it will surely come, it will not tarry.

What have you given up to strengthen your relationship with God?

Name a Bible verse that has carried you through rough seasons?

_____

_____

_____

_____

_____

_____

_____

_____

_____

_____

_____

_____

The Journey / The Path

Share a miracle that God performed for you?

_____

_____

_____

_____

_____

_____

_____

_____

_____

_____

_____

_____

Name a low point and remember how God came through for you?

_____

_____

_____

_____

_____

_____

_____

_____

_____

_____

_____

What new awareness from reading the book do you have about your personal journey?

_____

_____

_____

_____

_____

_____

_____

_____

_____

_____

CPSIA information can be obtained
at www.ICGtesting.com
Printed in the USA
JSHW050434170721
16999JS00004B/16